AIRPLANES

TRAVELING MACHINES

Jason Cooper

Rourke Enterprises, Inc.
Vero Beach, Florida 32964

PHOTO CREDITS

© Lynn M. Stone: pages 4, 8, 10, 15, 17, 21, and cover;
© Jerry Hennen: pages 7 and 12;
© Emil Punter/Photo Vision: pages 13, 18, and title page

LIBRARY OF CONGRESS
Library of Congress Cataloging-in-Publication Data
Cooper, Jason, 1942-
   Airplanes / by Jason Cooper.
   p. cm. — (Traveling machines)
   Includes index.
   Summary: Examines the history, varieties, and uses of
airplanes.
   ISBN 0-86592-493-7
   1. Airplanes—Juvenile literature. [1. Airplanes.] I. Series:
Cooper, Jason, 1942-   Traveling machines.
TL547.C66   1991
629.133'34—dc20   90-26925
                    CIP
                    AC

Printed in the USA

TABLE OF CONTENTS

Airplanes   5
The First Airplanes   6
Early Airplanes   9
Modern Airplanes   11
Light Planes   14
Airliners   16
Warplanes   19
Seaplanes   20
The Wonder of Airplanes   22
Glossary   23
Index   24

AIRPLANES

Airplanes are the fastest means of transportation on earth. An airplane can fly across the United States in under five hours.

Airplanes fly because they have wings for lift and engines for power.

An airplane body, or **fuselage,** is a hollow metal tube. Wings, tail, and **landing gear** are attached to the fuselage.

Moveable parts in the tail and wings control an airplane's height and direction.

Boeing 727 jet airliner

THE FIRST AIRPLANES

The first airplanes were made of wood, wire, and cloth. Orville and Wilbur Wright made the first airplane flight on December 17, 1903 at Kitty Hawk, North Carolina.

The Wrights' flight lasted only a few moments. But better airplanes were soon made. Several new airplanes were designed for use in World War I (1914-1918). Germany built a metal plane, and by war's end some planes could fly 130 miles per hour.

*German Fokker triplane
of World War I*

EARLY AIRPLANES

After World War I, bigger and faster airplanes were built. Airplanes also became safer, and people began to trust airplanes more.

An early success was the Ford Trimotor, a three-engined airplane. It could fly 100 miles per hour and carry 10 passengers. Another successful plane was the Douglas DC-3, first built in 1936. It became a favorite of the world's new **airlines.** A few DC-3s are still being flown.

Ford Trimotor of 1928

MODERN AIRPLANES

Late in World War II (1939-1945), the first **jet** airplanes appeared. True jets do not have **propellers,** and their engines thrust the planes at great speeds. Jets travel much faster than propeller-driven airplanes.

In the late 1950s and early 1960s, jet airplanes rapidly replaced the big propeller-driven passenger planes. Big jets fly over 500 miles per hour. The supersonic transports (SSTs) of Europe and Russia fly over 1,500 miles per hour!

Boeing 767, one of the newest jet airliners

U.S. Air Force F-16 Falcon fighters

Douglas DC-3 of the 1930s

LIGHT PLANES

Not all modern planes are jets. Most airplanes in the United States have one engine, and it is a propeller-driven engine. These are lightweight planes that can land at small airports.

Larger lightweight planes have two engines and can haul several people. Some of these airplanes are jet-powered.

Lightweight planes are used for many purposes: checking pipelines, photography, company business, and pleasure flights.

Piper Warrior

AIRLINERS

Large passenger planes are called airliners. These planes are owned by many different airlines, such as American, Delta, British, and United.

Most airliners carry 100 to 200 passengers at heights of 30,000 to 45,000 feet above the earth.

The biggest airliners—wide-bodied jumbo jets— carry as many as 500 passengers. The first jumbo jet was the huge four-engined Boeing 747 first flown in service in 1970. It is still the world's largest airliner.

Boeing 747, world's largest airliner

WARPLANES

Warplanes, or **military** planes, are armed with guns, bombs, or other weapons. They are usually used to attack ships, other planes, or targets on the ground.

The first warplanes fought in World War I. Twenty-five years later, in World War II, warplanes were extremely important in deciding battles.

Modern warplanes are fast, sleek jets. Some travel at 2,000 miles per hour—1,600 miles per hour faster than most World War II planes.

Boeing B-17 Flying Fortress bomber of World War II

SEAPLANES

Planes that can land and take off on water are seaplanes, or floatplanes. A seaplane floats on flat-bottomed structures called **pontoons.** In place of wheels, pontoons are attached to seaplane bodies.

Amphibians are planes that have wheels and pontoons. Like true amphibians—frogs and toads—these planes are at home on land or water.

Cessna Skyhawk with pontoons

THE WONDER OF AIRPLANES

Ask any pilot, and he or she will tell you that flying is an exciting way to travel.

Most airplane passengers feel the same way. With a surge of power, airplanes take people up into a completely different world.

Airplanes make travel quick and comfortable. They also offer a wonderful, bird's-eye view of the earth below. More important, airplanes have made our big world much smaller for everyone who flies.

Glossary

airline (AIR line) — a company that owns and operates airplanes for passenger and freight service

amphibian (am FIB ee en) — an airplane equipped with pontoons and wheels for use on both land and water

fuselage (FEWSS eh lajz) — the body of an airplane

jet (JET) — an airplane that uses jet engines

landing gear (LAN ding geer) — the structures under a plane—braces, tires, floats—that support it when it lands

military (MILL ah tary) — relating to war; military airplanes are designed for warfare

pontoon (pon TOON) — a float mounted under an airplane

propeller (pro PELL er) — a long, flat, turning blade mounted on some airplane engines to help pull the plane forward

INDEX

airliner   16

airlines   9, 16

amphibian   20

Boeing 747   16

Douglas DC-3   9

flight
  first   6
  height of   16

Ford Trimotor   9

fuselage   5

jet   11, 14, 16, 19
  jumbo   16

landing gear   5

passengers   9, 16, 22

pilot   22

pontoon   20

propeller   11, 14

seaplane   20

speed   6, 9, 11, 19

supersonic transport (SST)   11

tail   5

warplane   19

wings   5

World War I   6, 9, 19

World War II   19

Wright, Orville   6

Wright, Wilbur   6